SCOOBY-DOO!™

and the Truth Behind

SEA MONSTERS

BY TERRY COLLINS

ILLUSTRATED BY DARIO BRIZUELA

CAPSTONE PRESS
a capstone imprint

Published in 2015 by Capstone Press,
A Capstone Imprint
1710 Roe Crest Drive
North Mankato, Minnesota 56003
www.capstonepub.com

CAPS33088

Library of Congress Cataloging-in-Publication Data
Collins, Terry (Terry Lee), author.
Scooby-Doo! and the truth behind sea monsters /
by Terry Collins ; illustrated by Dario Brizuela.
pages cm. —— (Unmasking monsters with Scooby-Doo!)
Summary: "The popular Scooby-Doo! and the Mystery Inc. gang
teach kids all about sea monsters"—— Provided by publisher.
Audience: Ages 6–8.
Audience: K to grade 3.
Includes bibliographical references and index.
ISBN 978-1-4914-1793-5 (library binding)
1. Sea monsters——Juvenile literature. 2. Monsters——Juvenile
literature. 3. Curiosities and wonders——Juvenile literature.
I. Brizuela, Dario, illustrator. II. Title. III. Title: Sea monsters.
GR910.C56 2015
001.944——dc23   2014029121

Editorial Credits:
Editor: Shelly Lyons
Designer: Ted Williams
Art Director: Nathan Gassman
Production Specialist: Tori Abraham

Design Elements:
Shutterstock: ailin1, AllAnd, hugolacasse, Studiojumpee

The illustrations in this book were created traditionally,
with digital coloring.

Thanks to our adviser for her expertise, research,
and advice:
Elizabeth Tucker Gould, Professor of English
Binghamton University

Printed in the United States of America in
Stevens Point, Wisconsin
092014   008479WZS15

The weather at the beach was beautiful. Velma opened the picnic cooler. "Lunch time, gang!" she yelled. "Hey, where's Scooby?"

"No sign of him here!" Shaggy replied.

"He's not on the beach," Fred said.

"Scooby-Doo, where are you?" Daphne called toward the ocean.

"Rover here!" Scooby cried.

"Like, you totally crushed my castle, Scoob," said Shaggy.

Scooby pointed toward the water. "Rea ronster!" he yelled.

"So how big do sea monsters get, anyway?" Shaggy wondered.

"Well, the Leviathan was one of the biggest sea creatures of legend," said Fred. "One report had him being 900 miles (1,448 kilometers) long!"

"I'm sorry I asked," Shaggy said.

"He had rows of sharp teeth," Fred continued, "and breathed fire."

"Yikes!" said Scooby.

"So what's the most famous sea monster?" Shaggy asked.

"That's easy," replied Daphne. "The Loch Ness monster, or Nessie."

"Ressie?" asked Scooby.

Nessie has a small head and a long neck. She also has at least one hump on her back. Tourists from all around the world travel to Loch Ness in Scotland to try and see her. But Nessie has never been caught. Some people think she's a myth.

"So, have sea monsters ever attacked people?" Shaggy asked.

"Some of them, yes," Velma replied. "The mythical kraken was probably based on the real giant squid that still live today. The kraken lived off the coasts of Norway and Greenland. It grew up to 50 feet (15 m) long."

"Rig rea ronster!" Scooby said.

"Very big," said Fred. "With eight long arms, it was said to easily grab ships and pull them under water."

"Yes," said Velma. "It lives in and around the Congo River in Africa."

"No one has ever gotten a picture or any proof of the monster," Fred added. "But experts think it could be a long-lost dinosaur."

"It's said to have the body of an elephant and a long, flexible neck and tail," said Velma.

"According to the crew of the *Kuranda*, yes!" Velma said. "In 1973 a giant jellyfish got stuck to the front of their ship."

"How big was it?" Shaggy wondered.

"It weighed about 20 tons (18 metric tons)," said Velma, as she showed the gang the screen. "The tentacles were more than 200 feet (61 m) long."

"What should I do if I see a sea monster?" Shaggy asked.

"If you can, take pictures or video of what you see," Daphne replied.

"Yes," said Fred, "and try to get a good shot. The pictures people have taken of the Loch Ness monster are blurry and dark."

GLOSSARY

legend—a story passed down through the years that may not be completely true

myth—a story told by people in ancient times; myths often tried to explain natural events

mythical—imaginary or possibly not real

squid—a sea animal with a long, soft body and 10 fingerlike arms used to grasp food

tentacle—a long, flexible limb used for moving, feeling, and grabbing

venom—a poisonous liquid produced by some animals

READ MORE

Cerullo, Mary M. with Clyde F.E. Roper. *Giant Squid.* Searching for a Sea Monster. Smithsonian. North Mankato, Minn.: Capstone Press, 2012.

Veitch, Catherine. *Sea Monsters.* Legends of the Sea. Chicago: Raintree, 2010.

INDEX

Dunkleosteus, 7

fossils, 6

Hydra, 15

jellyfishes, 18—19

kraken, 12

Leviathan, 8

Loch Ness
monster, 10—11,
20

Mokele-mbembe,
16—17

Ogopogo, 14

Pterygotus, 7

taking pictures, 17,
20, 21

INTERNET SITES

FactHound offers a safe, fun way to find Internet sites related to this book. All of the sites on FactHound have been researched by our staff.

Here's all you do:

Visit *www.facthound.com*

Type in this code: 9781491417935

 **Super-cool stuff!** Check out projects, games and lots more at **www.capstonekids.com**